Let's go—

"Somewhere Else"

Richard Myers

Printed in Victoria, Canada

National Library of Canada Cataloguing in Publication Data

Myers, Richard
    Let's go - "somewhere else" / written by Richard Myers ; illustrated by Jay Wegter.
ISBN 1-4120-0608-2
    I. Title.
PS3613.Y47.L47 2003   811'.6   C2003-903500-X

TRAFFORD

This book was published *on-demand* in cooperation with Trafford Publishing.
On-demand publishing is a unique process and service of making a book available for retail sale to the public taking advantage of on-demand manufacturing and Internet marketing. **On-demand publishing** includes promotions, retail sales, manufacturing, order fulfilment, accounting and collecting royalties on behalf of the author.

Suite 6E, 2333 Government St., Victoria, B.C. V8T 4P4, CANADA
Phone   250-383-6864   Toll-free 1-888-232-4444 (Canada & US)
Fax   250-383-6804   E-mail   sales@trafford.com
Web site www.trafford.com   TRAFFORD PUBLISHING IS A DIVISION OF TRAFFORD HOLDINGS LTD.
Trafford Catalogue #03-0978   www.trafford.com/robots/03-0978.html

10   9   8   7   6   5   4

Let's go—

"Somewhere Else"

Poems
by
Richard Myers

Illustrated by Jay Wegter

To Joy

Many thanks to my Tuesday and Thursday writers for their suggestions and encouragement. A special thanks to Don Jennings for his patience and technical assistance.

R M

The road to "Somewhere Else" has no bumps or potholes; it is smoothly paved and easily traveled.

On your journey you will see people and places and things that may seem familiar, but curiously different. You may even recognize yourself.

It's a fun filled frolic that begins over the edge of this page. The light is green. Enjoy your trip.

R M

BILLY

My friend Billy
Is quite a fellow,
He'd never shout
Or ever bellow.
He's never mean
Or ever cross,
He never tries
To be the boss.
He's just as nice
As he can be,
He's a bit like you,
But more like me.

INNOCENT

I didn't break the window
Or muddy up the floor.
I didn't leave the water on
Or crack the kitchen door.
I didn't pour the catsup
On the baby in his pen.
I didn't crayon all the walls,
And I'll never do it again.

TRAPEZE ARTIST

He floats through the air
With the greatest of ease,
But I fear for the man
On the flying trapeze.

He may please the crowd
With his daring and flair,
But what if a sneeze
Should occur in the air?

There could be a time,
More horrible and grim,
If the need for a bathroom
Should fall upon him.

He may relish applause,
And the fame he has found,
But I prefer keeping
Both feet on the ground.

BROTHERS

Everyone should have a brother,
They're helpful and they're handy.
Whenever I'm in trouble,
I blame it all on Andy.

When mud is tracked upon the floor
And I'm questioned by my mother,
I never even bat an eye,
I blame it all on Brother.

Yes, a brother is a real help
Whenever there's a mess,
'Cause when there are two brothers,
Parents have to guess.

But if you have no brother,
Here's a plan to help you win:
Get yourself a little cat
And blame everything on him.

WONDERING

Some things are true,
And some things are not.
Does a humming bird hum?
Is a firefly hot?
Do raindrops catch cold
Before they are snow?
Will the candle go out
If there's no one to blow?
These things make me wonder,
But I haven't a clue.
I'm searching for answers,
How about you?

SLIM VIEW

My dad has chateaubriand,
A banquet, every dinner.
Mom endures the low-cal plates,
So how come Dad gets thinner?

CALL THE EXPERT

I just can't get this whatchamacallit
To stay the way it should.
If I had my gizmo with me,
Then perhaps I could.

What I need is a thingamajig,
But they're not commonplace.
The one I had for many years
Vanished without a trace.

I guess I need an expert
To get this thing to stay in place
I'll give a call to that know-it-all
Mr. Whatshisface.

PETER POTTER PALMINARY

Peter Potter Palminary
Is a name I like to hear,
I don't know why it happens,
But it fills me full of cheer.

Peter Potter Palminary
Is music to my ears,
A sweet recurring melody,
I've been hearing it for years.

Peter Potter Palminary
Rolls smoothly off the tongue,
Say it to yourself and see
It sounds like its been sung.

Peter Potter Palminary
Has nine years of history,
Today is my ninth birthday
And that name belongs to me.

PLAYMATE

Okay, okay, okay, okay,
If you really want me to I'll play,
Checkers, Chess, and some Scrabble,
But at times I just might babble.
For as you see the games unfold,
Please remember I'm three years old.

PROBLEM SOLVER

I bring to you this problem
For I have great resolve,
And I've heard there is no problem
That you find hard to solve.

You've mastered many mysteries
Of our endless universe,
So I know that you can rid me
Of this all too constant curse.

Tell me how to manage,
With help or all alone,
To get my sister to hang up
When she's on the telephone.

SLOW DOWN

We are all of us in a hurry.
There is little doubt about that.
The world would come to an end, I'm sure,
If we just stayed home and sat.

Why can't we take it easy,
Relax and lie around.
There are so many things to put off each day—
Opportunities abound.

I guess I'll start it by myself,
Begin a brand new trend.
Slow down, slow down, slow down, slow down,
I'll just sit on my end.

I'll start first thing tomorrow
To stop this rushing fuss.
I would have started it right now,
But I have to catch a bus.

SUING THE SOURCE

I'd lose some weight
  But I just hate
  Diets that are awful.
  As a last resort
   I'll go to court
    Food should be unlawful.

HOMEWORK

"An earthquake hit our house last night
It was an awful feeling,
I grabbed my mom and held on tight,
Some things fell from the ceiling.
Every windowpane was shattered
All the furniture was trashed,
Hanging pictures were now scattered
Every single thing just crashed."

That's the story I told Teacher,
And I'm sticking to it.
It's the story of my homework,
And why I didn't do it

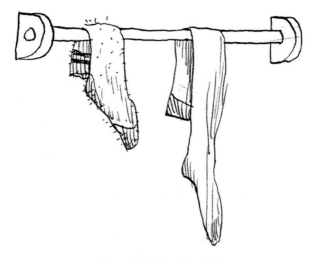

MISSING MATES

We are secretive socks and hideaway hose,
We find places to hide that nobody knows.
We cling to the walls of the dryer so tight,
In the dryer we are clean out of sight.

In a washer we have a trick that's much better,
We fold ourselves up and hide in a sweater.
Our owner won't find us, she can stand on her head,
Right now we are hiding under her bed.

Why we hide is not clear, but we'd like to state
Our hiding has nothing to do with our mate.
We'd like to be considered a pair,
Two of a kind seems right and seems fair.

But our fate is to be forever divisible
'Cause one of us always remains quite invisible.
Each person must have, as everyone knows,
Secretive socks and hideaway hose.

TRAVEL BABBLE

If I could travel anywhere,
And I know someday I will,
I'd go where the weather's fair,
And the rivers run uphill.
The people would be friendly,
They'd greet me with a smile,
Shake my hand and warmly say,
"Please stay with us awhile."
I don't know when I'll get there,
Or if it's far or near,
I've never been there before,
And I'm going again next year.

INVITATION

You're invited to come visit,
But not in winter time,
The days are frosty freezing,
Our stubborn sun won't shine.

Do stay away in summertime,
That's when we are on "bake."
The sun is stuck on sizzle,
It dries up every lake.

If you're thinking of the springtime,
Please plan on getting wet.
In spring we're always flooded,
A fact we all regret.

The weather's unpredictable,
Our problem in the fall,
Tornadoes, wind, hail, and sleet,
We have them one and all.

We retract our invitation.
It's an act that makes us blue,
But the weather here is rotten
So we will visit you.

SOMEWHERE ELSE

I'm going, I'm going,
I'm going somewhere,
I cannot stay here,
The climate's unfair.
Here's not the place
To be not at all,
It snows in July
And it's hot in the fall.
There must be a place
Where the weather is nice—
If I find such a place
I'm moving there twice.

GARDEN DIET

Garden bugs are so much fun
Some hop, some fly, and others run.
And if you keep a sharpened eye
You may appreciate the butterfly,
See the cricket in the grass,
And watch the hornet make a pass.
Perhaps I'll catch them, if I can,
And put them in a frying pan.
They'll make a perfect garden stew,
But I won't eat it, how about you?

BABY SITTING
(Here's what happened)

Coloring, painting, Pick-Up-Sticks,
Candy, cookies, magic tricks,
Football, baseball, and TV,
This kid will get the best of me.

I've cooked his dinner,
Made sure he's fed,
Thank goodness
It is time for bed.

But he won't stay
There in his bed.
He wants to play
Some more instead.

I can't keep up;
He just keeps going.
Will he get tired?
There's just no knowing.

When all was finally
Done and said,
He stayed up.
I went to bed.

SNOOPIES

The snoopies are coming,
You'd better beware,
The snoopies are coming,
You'd better take care.

They'll hide in the attic,
They'll hide in the hall,
They are so sneaky
They'll hide in the wall.

They have to hide
For it's very well known,
When snoopies come by
Your privacy's blown.

The job of all snoopies,
If they ever get through,
Is to tell everybody
The things that you do.

When snoopies are present
You'd better think twice,
Do everything pleasant
And everything nice.

We had some snoopies
But we knew what to do,
We acted just perfect
And sent them to you.

FROM HEAD TO TOE

I'm three years old
And grownups puzzle me.
They shouldn't act so strangely
For they're older, don't you see?
Whenever I go anywhere
They always look and stop and stare,
They point and laugh and even shout,
Every time that I go out.
Maybe it's the way I'm dressed.
I wear the hat I like the best.
I wear my best shoes too.
I think that's enough. Don't you?

TRICYCLE TROUBLE

I bought my son a tricycle
For his birthday, he was four.
I saw it in the window
Of our local hardware store.
"Easy to assemble,"
The sign had read so plain,
But instructions for assembly
Almost drove me quite insane.
The box contained many parts
Of every shape and size,
But when I checked the drawing
There were few to recognize.
Nothing that I tried was right,
Nuts and bolts would not get tight,
Still I worked into the night,
I've never been in such a plight.
Ten hours I did struggle,
It seemed to have me beat,
I've never been a quitter,
But I was near defeat.

Oh, I got it all together,
But it never quite resembled
The tricycle he's riding now,
I bought it—*pre-assembled.*

FLIGHT

The pilot is gone
And so is the crew,
I'm not getting on board
And neither should you.

CLOWNING AROUND

Eight-year-old Willie Brown
Wants to grow up to be a clown
With long shoes, a fat red nose,
Funny hair and enormous toes.

I wonder why Willie Brown
Wants to grow up to be a clown.
Why so strong an inclination
For that peculiar occupation?

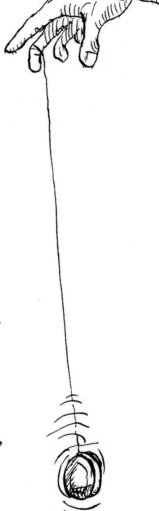

YO YO

I love playing with my yo yo.
I throw it up and down.
I play with it at home,
And I play with it in town.

I play with it at breakfast.
I play with it at night.
I really love my yo yo,
And I play with all my might.

If there's homework I should do,
You know it won't get done,
Because playing with my yo yo
Is fun, is fun, is fun.

I love "Rock the Cradle,"
And I'm great at "Walk the Dog,"
A million spins a year I think
Is what I finally log.

I don't know why I do it,
But I cannot stop this thing,
Perhaps it's not the yo yo—
Maybe it's the string.

TELEPHONE TROUBLE

One night when I was quite alone
I started playing with the phone.
I called New York and London too,
Next I called the Hamburg Zoo.
Punching numbers was so enthralling
I didn't care where I was calling.
Dad won't be pleased with me
When he hears from A.T.&T.
But it could have been much worse, you know,
I could have called The Home Shopping Show.

DON'T RUSH HER

Mom's found a new reducing plan,
A brand new kind of diet,
As soon as all her pizza's gone
I'm sure she's gonna try it.

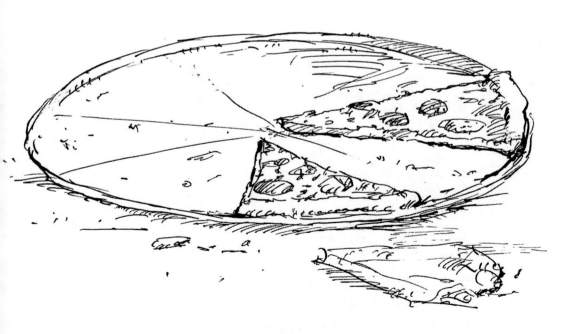

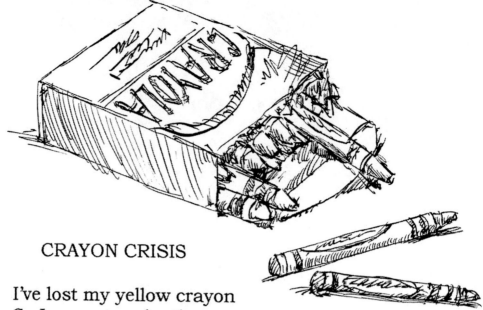

CRAYON CRISIS

I've lost my yellow crayon
So I cannot make the sun.
I have almost all my crayons,
But not the yellow one.

A picture needs a yellow sun
To brighten up the day,
Without a yellow sun it seems
Colored pictures aren't okay.

Johnny makes his suns with orange,
But that doesn't seem quite right,
Orange suns appear at twilight
When it is almost night.

That gives me an idea.
I'll make a picture of the night.
I won't need my yellow crayon,
No sun will be in sight.

I'll turn my picture over
And make a new one on the back,
I'll show how things look at night,
Good grief! I don't have black.

MR. PERFECT

I think that I shall never see
A person quite as nice as me,
A chap whose every spoken word
Is kind and soothing when it's heard,
A friend who gives a helping hand
With style and grace that's simply grand,
One whose things are gladly lent,
A staunch supporter heaven sent.
All these things come naturally
For the only perfect one is me.

WHAT ARE THESE THINGS?

I see them in the morning,
I see them in the night,
I see them when I'm in my bed,
They give me quite a fright.

I see them when they're standing
Very very tall.
I see them when they're sitting
Very very small.

I see them when they're flying
Smoothly through the air.
I see them when they're walking
Almost anywhere.

I see them when I'm drowsy,
And when I'm wide awake.
I'm getting kinda tired of them,
I am for goodness sake.

I see them when I'm happy,
And when I'm feeling sad.
They won't leave me alone,
I'm starting to get mad.

I know someday they'll go away,
But I don't know just when,
I have no idea what they are,
But here they come again!

BASEBALL HERO

He hits the ball way out of sight.
His speed is like a jet in flight.
He makes the fans all stand and scream,
Too bad he's on the other team.

PIRATES

He's Blackbeard the Pirate,
And I'm Pegleg Pete,
The toughest sea dogs
You ever will meet.

We're mean and nasty,
Slippery and cruel,
Throughout our domain
We ruthlessly rule.

If you cross our path,
It's curtains for you.
You'll be beggin' for mercy
Before we get through.

You might walk the plank,
Or be bound up in chain,
But one thing is certain,
We'll cause you some pain.

We've been pirates for years.
You could join us perhaps,
Mommy lets us be pirates
Right after our naps.

SAFE BELOW

Why is it when I'm in my bed
I see things I fear and dread?
I hear things that creep and crawl,
They do their crawling in the hall.
I will not scream; I will not cry.
There must be something I can try.
I've checked, it's clear beneath my bed,
I think that I'll sleep there instead.

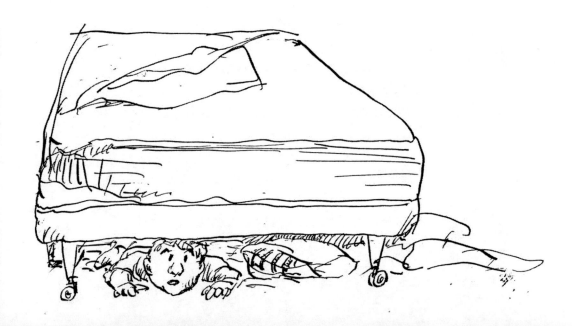

DEEP

The ocean floor has creatures galore
And they put on quite a show.
Each cucumber seems to slumber
And the jellyfish all glow.

The sea horses have no riders.
They never ever run.
They jump and hop and float about
Watching them is fun.

A giant clam is yawning
Its mouth a great big gap
If something comes too close it will
Make a giant SNAP.

There are octopus and urchin,
Crabs and even eels,
And if you chance to touch them
Strange is how it feels.

But the little squid, that I call Sid,
Is the strangest of the lot,
For when he's right in front of you,
Suddenly he's not.

CELEBRATION

Did you ever have a day
When everything goes crazy?
I think I had one yesterday
But my memory is hazy.

When I awoke in my bed
The darkness seemed so bright,
Sun streaked through the window
In the middle of the night.

Everything was topsy-turvy,
Nothing seemed quite right.
My stomach told me I was sick.
I know I looked a fright.

I'm sure the cause was what I ate
When I was on the town.
I hope things return to normal
'Cause I'm feeling upside down.

TOO HUNGRY

I'm waiting for the locksmith.
I've been waiting for some time.
I'm getting very hungry,
It is no fault of mine.

Just about a week ago
Mom gained a bit more weight.
She did it on her diet, number
One hundred-fifty-eight.

She eats a bit of everything,
Then looks around for more,
She has sampled every item
In our local grocery store.

She nibbles, munches, gobbles, chews;
She never will be thin.
It's a battle she just has to lose,
A war she cannot win.

She cannot stop her eating
Almost everything in sight,
Dad had a great idea,
But it didn't work out right.

Oh locksmith please get here soon,
I am begging, please oh please,
I knew we were in trouble
When Mommy ate the keys.

MY PET SNAIL

I have a pet snail named Moe.
Snails aren't very fast, you know.
He cannot run but he can glide
Around my backyard countryside.
You may think a snail's a pet
That people shouldn't ever get,
But Moe's the best pet there can be,
He never runs away from me,
He doesn't bark and never bites,
And never ever gets in fights.
The bestest thing about my Moe
Is I can catch him 'cause he's slow.

SOMETHING NEW

Today I decided to try something new
So I took a long ride on a kangaroo,
Went down to the ocean and hopped on a whale
And off we went for a hundred-mile sail.
Then I managed a trip on someone's lost kite
And rode it all night till my house came in sight.
The day was exciting and daring and bold,
But tomorrow I think I'll try something old!

SOMETHING SCARY

There's something scary through that door,
It's dark and I can't see.
There's something scary through that door,
And it really bothers me.
There's something scary through that door,
It might be big or small.
There's something scary through that door,
It might walk or crawl
There's something scary through the door,
But I don't know just what.
There's something scary through that door,
I think I'll keep it shut.

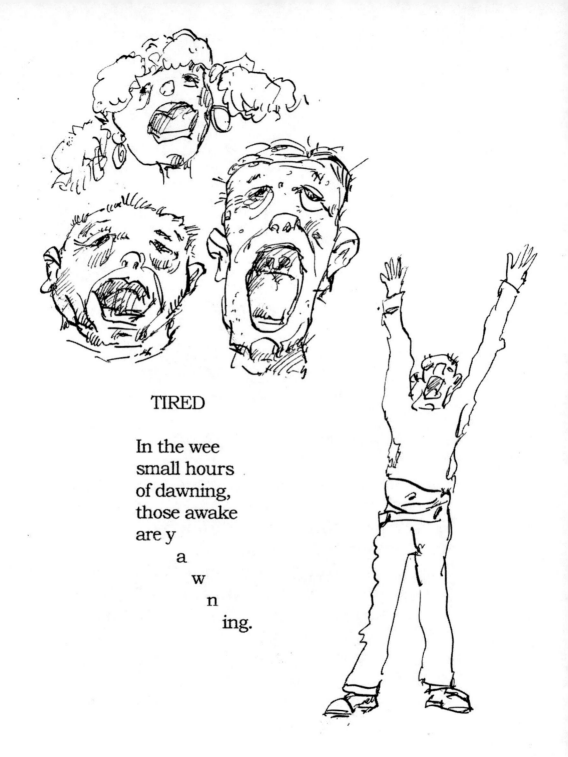

TIRED

In the wee
small hours
of dawning,
those awake
are y
      a
        w
          n
            ing.

SOCKS

Who makes these socks?
They do not fit me right.
The foot is way too loose
And the top is far too tight.

Why do little balls of thread
Irritate my toes?
Who makes these socks?
Is there someone here who knows?

Sock makers really should
Be very much aware,
That coverings for footsies
Should be made with greater care.

I will not put them on again;
With these socks I'm through.
They are so uncomfortable
I'm giving them to you.

GOOD ADVICE

Never put off
   what you have to do.
Never take many,
   you can do with a few.
Never spend all,
   but save some for later.
Never think small,
   try to think greater.
Never be mean
   when you can be nice.
Never, no never,
   give any advice.

ELEPHANTS DON'T ROLLER SKATE

Elephants don't roller skate,
Polar bears won't dance,
Giraffes don't ride bicycles,
Even if they have the chance.

Squirrels do not play football,
Donkeys won't chop wood,
Moths won't stay away from lights
Though probably they should.

Catfish don't play tennis,
Antelope won't drive a truck,
Sharks don't play Monopoly,
You won't hear an eagle cluck.

Rabbits don't eat spaghetti,
Guinea pigs won't mountain climb,
Beavers don't plant gardens
Although they have the time.

Bears don't go to movies,
A deer won't climb a tree,
Cows will not give chocolate milk
And high dives are not for me.

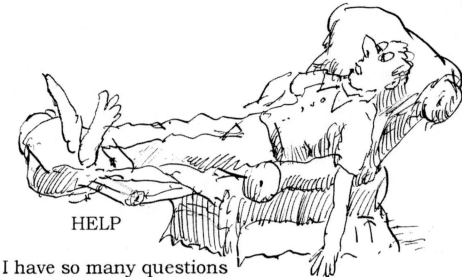

HELP

I have so many questions
That confound and puzzle me,
Help me find the answers
Is my never-ending plea.
What does a humming bird hum
If it doesn't know a tune?
How do four o'clock flowers know
When it is four past noon?
Why do potatoes all have eyes
When it's plain they cannot see?
Why do all these silly things
Always bother me?
If you know the answers,
Please help me in my quest,
Write them down somewhere for me,
I've got to get some rest.

ANIMAL CRACKERS

I'm going on safari,
Come on along with me,
There are many animals
That I'm sure we're bound to see.

There will, of course, be lions,
Giraffes, and monkeys too,
The safari that we'll go on
Is better than a zoo.

We'll get to see each animal
And touch them just for fun,
Better yet, we'll not be through
'Till we've eaten every one.

INCOMPLETE

I'm going out to play today,
No matter what the weather,
The first thing I must do, of course,
Is get my parts together.

My head goes on my neck, I've learned,
Now that I'm getting older,
And on my neck I next will put
My right and then left shoulder.

I'll go back to my head and add
A mouth and my two eyes,
Without them people would, I'm sure,
Be quick to criticize.

When I've fitted my arms and hands
I'll be very nearly done,
With my torso, my legs, and feet
I'll be able to skip and run.

Still I feel that something's missing,
I stuck on my ears and hair,
But I have this awful feeling
There's a part that isn't there.

I remembered all my fingers,
Added each of my ten toes,
But I'm sure that something's missing,
Is there someone here who knows?

CHILDREN'S BEDTIME

Why is it when it's time for bed
Thirsty thoughts come to his head?
He wants a drink, a glass or pitcher,
And, of course, so does his sister.

"One more time," I say to Mother,
"You tell her, I'll tell her brother,
If out of them there's one more peep
They stay up. We go to sleep!"

ELEPHANT PARTY

The elephants had a party,
They came from far and wide,
The ground did shake and rumble,
Other animals tried to hide.

The ants did not know what to do,
They scrambled to and fro,
Each one trying frantically
To dodge an elephant's toe.

Monkeys climbed up in the trees
And began a lively chatter.
Moles looked out from darkened holes
To see what was the matter.

They quickly called a meeting
Of all the other animals about,
And came to the conclusion that
THE ELEPHANTS MUST GET OUT.

But who would tell the elephants
That they would have to leave?
The plan they made was simple
And quite easy to conceive.

They sent a little mouse to say,
"You are not wanted here."
One look at the messenger
And the elephants fled in fear.

DANCE CONTEST WINNER

She won the contest of the dance
Because of a strange circumstance.
You should have seen her spin and prance
When she found her pants were full of ants.

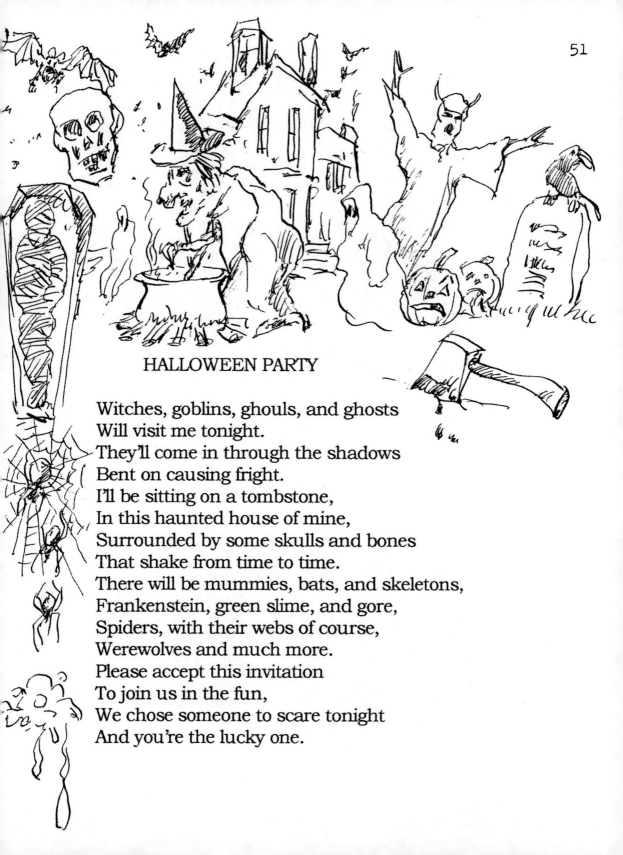

HALLOWEEN PARTY

Witches, goblins, ghouls, and ghosts
Will visit me tonight.
They'll come in through the shadows
Bent on causing fright.
I'll be sitting on a tombstone,
In this haunted house of mine,
Surrounded by some skulls and bones
That shake from time to time.
There will be mummies, bats, and skeletons,
Frankenstein, green slime, and gore,
Spiders, with their webs of course,
Werewolves and much more.
Please accept this invitation
To join us in the fun,
We chose someone to scare tonight
And you're the lucky one.

THE MAGICIAN

Prepare to be awed and possibly sawed
The magician is back in our town.
He does things to amaze, puts you in a daze,
The magician now back in our town.
His sleight of hand is utterly grand,
The magician now back in our town.
He pulls things from hats, rabbits and bats,
The magician now back in our town.
You'd better take care and you'd better beware
Of the magician now in our town.
He's been here before; it's more than folklore,
That he certainly should have been banished.
When his act was all done, we'd had wonderful fun,
But found that our money had vanished.

FOOLISH FRANK'S FIRE

Frank was eight and loved his sled
When the hills were full of snow,
And the colder that it got
The faster Frank would go.

He came home one day from sledding
Chilled right to the bone.
It was two degrees outside
He was glad to get back home.

He went into the cozy den
And built a roaring fire.
As he warmed up, he could see
The flames were getting higher.

Then Dad rushed in and Frank could see
Redness flush Dad's face,
"I told you Frank," he shouted,
"WE DON'T HAVE A FIREPLACE!"

THE INVISIBLE MAN

I didn't see the invisible man
When he came to my room last night,
I'm certain he was here because
He wasn't anywhere in sight.
I couldn't see a trace of him
Though I turned the lights on high,
He didn't ever say "Hello"
And he never said "Goodbye."

Why he came to my house
Remains a mystery,
He may frighten other kids,
But he doesn't bother me.
He and my Closet Monster
Played the games that spookies play,
I know some day, when I grow up,
They both will go away.

MAGICAL DAD

Mom says Dad is magic
He makes things disappear
He has a place for everything
But when he looks, *"It isn't here."*

Things just turn up missing,
Like the rake and garden shears,
Dad can't mow the lawn, of course,
The mower's been gone for years.

It doesn't matter what it is,
If it belongs to Dad,
Someday it will vanish
It makes me feel so sad.

Dad is not discouraged,
"There's a place where things should be."
But every time he finds that place
His things aren't there to see.

I'm starting to get worried,
For I fear eventually.
Dad will come a looking—
Looking just for me.

SUMMER SNOWMAN

We made a snowman out of hay
And we made him wide and tall
It was extremely hot that day
For it was far from fall.

With hat of sticks and corn cob nose
Our work was finally ended
Six feet high our snowman rose
He looked very splendid.

Some may say, "Snowman of hay?
You have to be out of your mind!"
But ours will never melt away
'Cause we made a different kind.

TRAVELER

Have you ever been to China,
Or Germany or Rome?
I'm going there tomorrow
Even though it's far from home.
From Rome I'll go to Singapore,
Then off to Timbuktu,
I'm certain that I'll like it,
And I know that you would too.
From Timbuktu I'll travel
To Switzerland and France,
I always knew I would go far
If I ever got the chance.
Should I go to far off Russia
Or Perhaps Brazil instead?
I'll decide tomorrow,
If I get out of my bed.

CHOOSING TEAMS

I dribble with great speed and skill,
And move smoothly down the court,
But they never pick me quickly;
They choose a different sort.

At free throws I am very good,
My three pointers often swish,
I always hope they'll chose me first,
But I never get my wish.

My passes are all straight and true,
The ball speeds hard and fast,
So how come when they're choosing,
They always choose me last?

BACK AND FORTH

There is something I don't understand,
It makes no sense to me:
How can things go back and forth?
They must first go forth you see.

Could an airplane make a landing
Before it was in the air?
I'm sure that you don't think so,
But maybe you don't care.

Could someone ever catch a ball
Before the ball was thrown?
The answer should be clear to all,
It shouldn't be unknown.

Forth and back I have no doubt
Is the way that things should be.
I hope you have it figured out,
And that you agree with me.

BALANCING MARY
(A Carnival Act)

Balancing Mary is something to see,
She balances things on top of her knee,
On her nose, on her elbow, even her toe,
The number of things continues to grow.
An apple, an orange, and then comes a chair,
She keeps piling them on; they rise in the air.
On top of her nose, a cockatoo bird,
On top of the bird, a peach pie—how absurd.

On her toe she has started other things going,
As she adds each new thing it is certainly growing:
There's a football, a table, and now a shoetree,
Then a lamp and a cane and, my gosh, now there's me.
I'm balancing here on the cane thanks to Mary,
And I have to admit that it is rather scary.
I'm not going to jump; it's too high that's a fact,
But I fear I'm now part of the sword thrower's act.

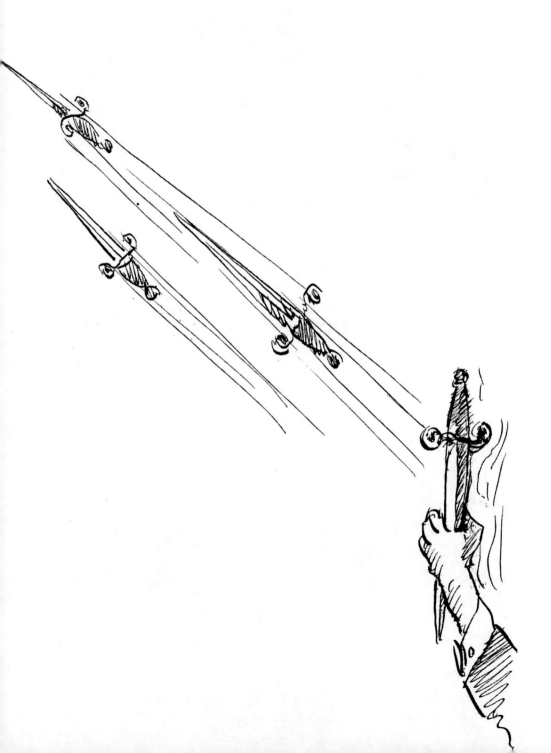

LIGHT FANTASTIC

Mom's found a new reducing plan
And I know that she will try it:
Spaghetti, spumoni, and pizza—
That's just her kind of diet.

HOUSEHOLD HELPER

Margaret is our live-in helper,
Some think she's quite terrific,
At all the jobs she does for us,
But let me be specific:

She vacuums all the carpets,
Polishes the silverware,
Washes all the dishes,
And dusts most everywhere.

She cooks breakfast, lunch, and dinner,
Sets the table, serves the meals,
She couldn't do it faster
Unless she were on wheels.

She does everybody's laundry,
Gets all windows clean and bright,
Makes each and every single bed,
Folds the sheets exactly right.

She's very good at mowing lawns,
Prunes the flowers so they'll grow,
She'll wash the car and shine it
'Till it has a wondrous glow.

But I don't think she works too hard.
For her I shed no tear,
'Cause each and every job she does,
She does but once a year.

BOYS' TOYS

Why do I and other boys
Have so many broken toys?
We have little horns that will not toot
And little guns that will not shoot,
Trains that don't go anywhere,
Balloons that won't float in the air,
Tiny cars that will not run,
That's no fun for anyone.

For little girls it's not that way.
Their toys all work when they're at play.
They play house with Ken and Barbie.
If you made me do that, you'd be sorry.
Girls like to play with tiny tea sets.
The more I think, the worse it gets.
And even though they'd gladly share,
I really really do not care,
'Cause I don't like their toys. (So there.)

BOYS ARE STRANGE

Boys make no sense at all.
Why do they throw and catch a ball,
Or run and jump and dance about
Yell, scream, bellow, shout?
They really do the strangest things.
I'm sure they'd fly if they had wings.

Girls make more sense, you know.
They like to bake; they like to sew.
They dress up and have some tea,
You never see them climb a tree.
When I grow up, perhaps then,
I'll understand boys when they're men.

SCHOOL TIME

You hear the children laugh and shout
The moment that their school is out.
They show their happy smiles and grins,
But not each day when school begins.

POSTAL SERVICE

I have to say, without a doubt,
I'm very anxious to get out,
My daddy said, "Go with the mail."
And now I'm in this postal jail.
I hope the mail is picked up quick,
I'm very warm and feeling sick,
The mailman will know what to do,
He'll send me home stamped—"Postage Due."

MR. RIGHT AND MR. WRONG

Said Mr. Right to Mr. Wrong,
"Why do you take so very long
to answer every single question
when I know that you're just guessin'.
You never ever get one right;
I do not understand your plight.
You take so long to guess and then
you answer wrongly once again.

Said Mr. Wrong to Mr. Right,
"I answer wrongly day and night
but not because I'm always guessin'
I never understand the question.
Confusion always has remained
'Cause questions never are explained.
This example I give to you:
Five plus five equals who?"

KEEP YOUR SHOES ON

One foot
   two feet
      three feet, four
         feet keep coming more and more.

Five feet
   six feet
      seven, ten
         another foot comes again and again.

Lookout!
   Beware!
      Take care, take heed,
         These marching feet bring the centipede.

Mr. SCHNEE

He's stingy and bossy,
Boastful and mean,
He's naughty and nasty,
Unkempt and unclean.

He talks and he talks,
There is never an end,
Nobody likes him,
He hasn't a friend.

I'd like to help him,
Really I would,
A person should help
Whenever he could.

I know that you feel
The way that I do,
So visit me Tuesday
And take him with you.

BROTHER'S ROOM

My brother's room is so untidy
Clothes are everywhere.
I never go into his room
'Cause something's in the air.
The windows are so full of grime
Through them the sun can never shine.
No other room is such a mess
Except, of course, there's mine. (I guess.)

NO PEAS PLEASE

I'll eat squash and broccoli,
Beets and spinach too,
But please, oh please, oh please,
Never ever give me peas.

Those little balls of vegetable
Jangle all my nerves
Because they never ever will,
Get on my plate and just sit still.

It's not that I don't like the taste
Whenever I must take some,
I find the taste of peas just great,
But they keep rolling off my plate.

COMPUTER RACE

Our two computers had a race,
It was the swiftest kind of pace,
The chips were down, circuits blazing,
To see it all was quite amazing.
Through the night each one speeded
Until the power was exceeded,
The fuses blew, the screens went gray,
Each mouse got scared and ran away.

NURSERY NONSENSE

Jack and Jill may have gone up the hill
But there is one thing I want to know—
Who builds a well at the top of a hill
When the water is down below?

Did Jack Horner sit in a corner?
I can't believe that it's true.
He couldn't sit, that's too tight a fit
Unless he were built quite askew.

And I don't want to knock that Dickery Dock
'Cause I know it was mostly for fun,
But what I want to know, is where did it go
When the mouse was on the run?

I may be insane but these rhymes seem inane,
To me every one is a riddle,
But they still bring cheer to every young ear,
So hail to Miss Muffet and High diddle diddle.

QUIETVILLE

I just got back from Quietville,
Things are different there.
People speak in whispers,
There's a hush that fills the air.

Dogs don't bark
And cows don't "Moo"
There's not a sound
To bother you.

Trains go by on tiptoe,
Cars glide down the street,
Church bells have no clappers,
It's a town that is unique.

They show only silent movies,
Every TV is on mute,
Popcorn doesn't really pop,
And horns there never toot.

It truly is a fine place,
And my visit there was swell,
But I'm glad to be back home because—
I'VE GOT THE URGE TO YELL!

QUESTIONS

Why can't ants move backwards
Do they have only forward gears?
If porcupines sat down
Would they move themselves to tears?
If elephants packed their trunks,
What would they put inside?
And when a hyena laughs,
Does it ever hurt its side?
When monkeys start to chatter,
Do they ever make much sense?
Why can't forests just once be bright,
I've always heard they're dense.
If a gazelle became quite clumsy,
Not as poised as all the rest,
Would it have to go to school
And pass a graceful test?
These questions may seem foolish,
But it's just the shape I'm in,
I don't have much to do, you see,
Here in my loony bin.

NOTHING TO DO

What do you do when there's nothing to do?
It's very hard work, don't you know.
It's almost as hard as going somewhere
When there isn't a where place to go.
If this problem seems perplexing,
Don't you worry, don't you pout,
Just put some nice new clothes on
And go out and walk about.

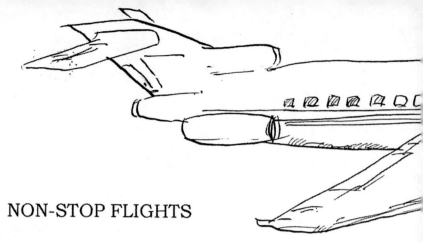

NON-STOP FLIGHTS

Never take a non-stop flight.
Heed my warning and beware,
Learn from my experience,
Read this notice and take care.

I was flying from Seattle
To Chicago, my home town,
I thought that when we got there,
The plane would then touch down.

I didn't know that "non-stop" meant
The plane is always flying.
I've been up here for two weeks now,
I cannot stop my crying.

The food has been all right, I guess,
And the flight attendant's cute,
But the only way to leave this plane
Is with a parachute.

I was terrified to try it,
But what else could I do?
So look out down below,
'Cause I might land on you.

SONS

"My son's driving me up the wall," said Bill.
I know exactly how he's feeling.
I have a son myself, you see,
He has me on the ceiling.

FOOLISH FRANK'S GARDEN

Frank cannot understand it.
His garden just won't grow.
He watered it and fed it,
And worked hard with the hoe.
It simply will not spring to life,
It gives him nothing more than strife,
Make it grow? He can't, he can't.
Could it be—he didn't plant?

DAYTIME RAIN

I hate it when it rains, don't you?
My outdoor fun is then all through.
I could go out but I'd get wet
Has it stopped raining? No, not yet.

I hope it stops so I can play
Tennis or perhaps croquet.
If I could make it rain just right
It wouldn't rain except at night.

I know that trees and flowers both
Need rain to help them with their growth
But I, for one, would have more fun
When in the daytime there is sun.

THE DENTIST

In my youth to him I ventured
So later I would not be dentured.
My latest visit made me proud,
I still cried, but not as loud.

NO DOUBT ABOUT IT

I am absolutely certain
The Tooth Fairy exists,
And don't tell me that Santa
Is one of many myths.

The Easter Bunny hides the eggs,
Of that there is no doubt,
There's a monster in the Lock Ness,
But he just won't come out.

Big Foot's good at hiding,
But still I know he's there,
And Cupid does shoot arrows
To create a loving pair.

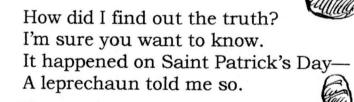

How did I find out the truth?
I'm sure you want to know.
It happened on Saint Patrick's Day—
A leprechaun told me so.

FUN TIME

Hooray, hooray, hooray, hooray,
The school bus didn't come today,
I guess I'll stay at home and play,
Hooray, hooray, hooray, hooray.

Mom's still sleeping,
Dad is too,
I think that's very strange
Don't you?

Hey, wait a minute, I remember,
There is no school 'till next September.
It's time for fun and relaxation,
School's okay, but I love vacation.

THE WICKED ITCH SISTERS

We're the wicked Itch Sisters, Susan and Daisy,
We give out the itches that drive people crazy.
Susan prefers to give itches gigantic,
She likes to see people scratch in a panic.

I give out itches so tiny and small
People can't find where to scratch them at all.
Sometimes we'll give an itch that seems glued,
The itch that we give depends on our mood.

There are times that we'll place an itch on a nose,
And times that we'll place them on somebody's toes.
Of course a good place for an itch is an ear,
Another good place is somebody's rear.

Yes, we're wicked Itch Sisters and we're full of glee,
It's a joy to give itches they're fun and they're free.
If you have no itches be happy today—
The wicked Itch Sisters are coming your way.

KING OF THE HILL

I'm king of the hill,
The master of mound,
I like it up here,
I may never come down.

This hill is just fine,
It's my private domain,
I think on this hill
I shall always reign.

I'll sleep on the ground,
I won't mind if it's hard,
This hill is all mine,
Every inch, every yard.

I'll need food and clothes
And a few other things
To make my domain
Fit for us kings.

To get what I need
I'll go into town,
When I figure out
How I can get down.

NIGHT ANIMALS

Strange animals visit me at night,
Why they come I do not know.
All the zebras have green stripes.
In the dark they flash and glow.

The flying hippopotamus
Is a graceful sight to see,
And the polka dotted cows
Never ever bother me.

These creatures often visit me
But I have no fear or dread,
I know that they will go away
When I get out of my bed.

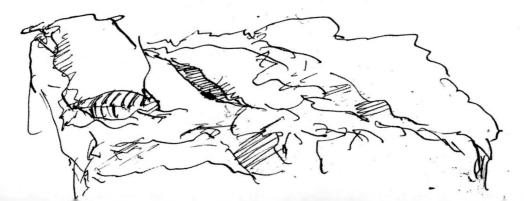

HEAVY BIRD

Mr. McGreader has a bird feeder
Perfect for sparrows and crows,
But a jay full of greed
Eats all of the seed...
How it flies nobody knows.

SOMEONE ELSE

I wish that I were someone else,
But who I can't decide,
Perhaps I should be Batman
With Robin by my side.

Superman would be okay,
I'd fly right through the air,
Or Spiderman and then I could
Climb almost anywhere.

Harry Potter would be fun,
And life would be so thrilling,
If I had the magic wand,
I'd be more than willing.

Dick Tracy might be dangerous,
But I'm certain quite exciting,
I'd be a member of the force,
And super at crime fighting.

This pondering has tired me
So I'll go back to bed.
Of all the people I could be,
I'll just be me instead.

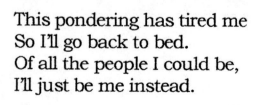

CHICKEN FEED

I'm awfully tired of chicken,
And I'll tell you why,
I have chicken every single day,
Even chicken pie.

I just can't look at chicken,
And believe me I have tried,
It doesn't matter how it's made
Boiled, baked, or fried.

Don't talk to me of chicken.
I know all about it, see,
That finger lickin' chicken
Is slowly killing me.

So here's my ultimatum,
You can be certain that
If they give me more chicken,
This cat is gonna scat.

ABETRIMLINSA ZIMKOVINOVITCH

His name is Abetrimlinsa Zimkovinovitch.
He's from some strange and distant land.
It has to be a place, I'm sure,
Where pronunciation isn't planned.

He's in our fourth grade class this year,
But when Teacher calls on him,
The name gives her no trouble,
She calls him Abe or Zim.

ANIMAL DIETS

When I see an elephant, I think he is elegant,
As he moves the ground goes CRUNCH!
I wonder why he is much bigger than me?
It's not the peanuts, that's my hunch.
And I pity the pelican with a hunger his belly can
Hardly manage all on his plate,
He flies low in the sky. Why can't he fly high?
I'm sure it was something he ate.
And I'm never oblivious to tigers carnivorous
As they strut in their cage, oh so quiet,
I don't go too near for I have a great fear
They'd like to add me to their diet.

MISS MUFFET AND THE SPIDER

If Little Miss Muffet sat on a tuffet,
She must have been little indeed.
I'm glad she left quicker
Than the spider could pick her
For a meal on which it could feed.

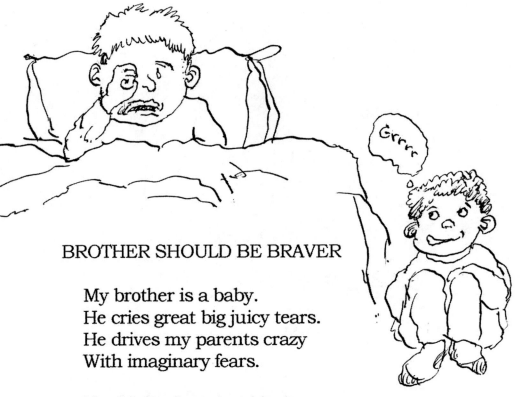

BROTHER SHOULD BE BRAVER

My brother is a baby.
He cries great big juicy tears.
He drives my parents crazy
With imaginary fears.

He thinks there is a blosit
Hissing in his closet,
And that a giant snapping schned
Is scratching underneath his bed.

I've never seen a blosit,
Perhaps it's something new.
I've never seen a snapping schned,
Not even in a zoo.

Brother should be braver,
For he's older don't you see.
He is almost five years old
And I am only three.

Someday soon I'll tell him,
Those things he cannot see,
Making all those noises,
Are noises made by me.

SHARING

I do not feel all that sick,
But my stomach's kind of queasy,
My tongue is very much too thick
And my nose is acting sneezy.

I'd like to go outside and play
But I'm not at my peak,
Why not come and visit me,
I've been inside all week.

We could play Monopoly
Or perhaps a game of Clue.
You really are my dearest friend
So I'll share my flu with you.

FAT CAT

My friend Billy has a cat
That's much too big and far too fat.
He cannot jump or catch a mouse,
He barely fits into the house.

It's sad to see a cat that can't
Run fast enough to catch an ant.
I do not know where Bill will buy it,
But he's got to get that cat a diet.

AUNT BERTHA

Aunt Bertha sometimes bothers me
Aunt Bertha says, "Don't climb that tree,
Don't jump, don't shout, and please don't run."
Sometimes Aunt Bertha's just no fun.

But every time I visit her
She is always in the kitchen.
Delicious chocolate cookies—
My favorite things she's fixin'.

So I don't climb, and I don't jump,
And I am careful not to run,
I hug Aunt Bertha warmly
And I eat cookies one by one.

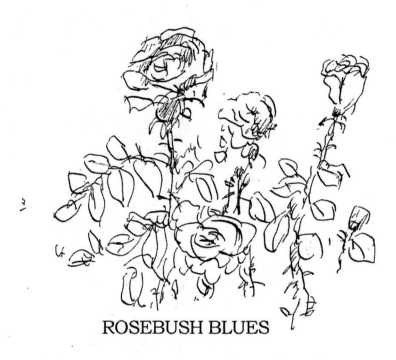

ROSEBUSH BLUES

It simply is grand to see rosebuds expand
All nature it seems is reborn,
But it's hard to be gay and think in that way
When your finger is stuck on a thorn.

I MADE MY MOMMY BREAKFAST

I made my mommy breakfast,
It was a big surprise,
She really did enjoy it,
I could see it in her eyes.

The omelet came out perfect,
I put flowers in for flavor,
She found it very tasty,
I could tell from her behavior.

She hugged me and she held me,
Gave me many many kisses,
And then she said, "Darling,
I just have two wishes."

She said she'd like to be the cook,
And make everything delicious,
Then when we're finished eating
She'd like me to do the dishes.

MR. ...?

He almost won the game today,
He almost lost it too,
He almost is a bit like me,
And he almost is like you.
He's almost always friendly,
And he's almost never mean,
He's almost always with us,
But he's almost never seen.
He's almost always different,
But he's almost quite the same,
He's the almost almost man,
And he almost has a name.

FOLLOWING

Emergency, emergency!
My kitty's stuck up in a tree
'Cause when I climbed
He followed me. Emergency.

Call the police and firemen too.
Have them bring a rescue crew
And when they free him from the tree
Have them do the same for me.

DON'T BOTHER THE GIRAFFE

The giraffe, I think, is very wise,
But he has a strange look in his eyes.
Is it caused by what he hears
In each of his enormous ears?
Or is it something that he sees
Through the leaves of taller trees?
It must be something in this zoo,
He can't see me. Can he see you?

ON THE WAY TO KINDERGARTEN

She saw a tiger yesterday,
On the way to school.
She ran away from him, of course,
She is nobody's fool.

A tiger's not supposed to be
Where children walk about.
She was so very frightened
She gave a terrible shout.

The tiger did not chase her,
On her he did not chew,
She feared she'd hear him roaring,
But instead she heard him "MOO."

ANT RACES

Bill and I and Paul and Vance
Decided we would race some ants.
We built a racetrack in a box
With running lanes and starting blocks.
We knew ants were rather slow
And wondered how fast they would go.
We put each ant right in its place
And Paul yelled, "GO" to start the race.
Racing ants for us was new
And we were glad when it was through.
It took hours and hours, about nine,
For those ants to reach the finish line.

SIGNIFICANT

The greatest thought
Of modern man
Must surely be,
"Yes I can."

The idea for "Non-Stop Flights" came from a George Carlin routine and I have to thank the late Victor Borge for "Foolish Frank's Fire."

A few of the late Milton Berle's jokes probably triggered a verse or two, but the rest I just imagined. *R W*

INDEX

ISBN 141200466-7